NATIONAL
GEOGRAPHIC

D0503589

Jamestown

PIONEER EDITION

By Fran Downey and Lana Costantini

CONTENTS

Remaking History. *This house is part of a museum. It shows what life was like in Jamestown around 1614.*

Celebrate Jamestown

By Fran Downey

WHAT EVENT WAS MOST IMPORTANT IN U.S. HISTORY? WAS IT THE AMERICAN REVOLUTION? WHAT ABOUT THE CIVIL WAR? THERE ARE MANY CHOICES.

Yet the founding of Jamestown may have mattered most. Everything in America changed after that—even worms. Why worms? Let's dig into the story of Jamestown to find out.

A Dangerous Land

It was May 14, 1607. That day, three ships came to shore near a riverbank. They **landed** in what is now Virginia. The people on the ships were from England. They wanted to start a new **colony**. They named it Jamestown.

Life there was hard, and the **colonists** feared attacks. England and Spain were at war. The colonists worried that Spanish soldiers might attack. The colonists also feared the nearby Native Americans, known as the Powhatan. To stay safe, the colonists built a wooden fort.

CANADA

U.S. — AREA OF MAP

Chesapeake Bay

ATLANTIC OCEAN

POWHATAN LAND

Jamestown →

- ☐ Powhatan Land
- ☐ River
- ☐ Swamp

New Home. *The first colonists land at Jamestown. It took five months to get there.*

Heading Home?

The colonists' real problem, though, was water. Little rain had fallen in a long time. Without water, crops did not grow. The colonists were often hungry. They even ate dogs and rats.

The colonists drank river water. The muddy, salty water made people ill. Many people died from that. Others died from hunger.

After nearly two years, the colonists were tired. They prepared to go home. Then supply ships arrived with food. The colony was saved!

Things started to get better. Rain came at last. So did new colonists.

A Better Life

One new colonist was John Rolfe. In 1614, he married a Native American named Pocahontas. Her father was the Powhatan's chief. Their marriage brought peace to the colony.

Rolfe also brought success to Jamestown. He showed colonists a new kind of tobacco. Growing it raised money for the colony.

Some people came to Jamestown against their will. Kidnappers brought enslaved people from Africa. Many worked in the tobacco fields. A few of these people were freed later. Jamestown did not offer everyone a better life.

A Changing Land

The colonists changed America a lot. They brought cattle, chickens, goats, horses, and pigs. These animals had not lived here before.

The colonists even brought worms.

Before 1607, worms were not found in some parts of America. The worms made big changes. They ate leaves off forest floors, so rain hit the ground. The rain washed away the best part of the soil. That made it hard for some plants to grow.

The colonists brought bees, too. Busy bees helped watermelons and fruit trees grow. They helped these and other new plants take root.

Success at Last!

Jamestown was the first English colony that lasted. It was a key part of American history. The colonists changed the land and helped make the America we know today.

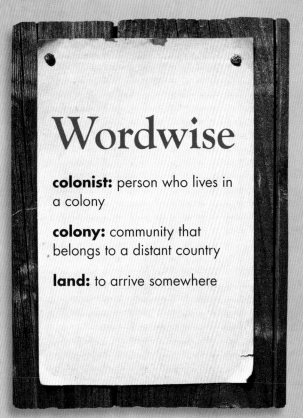

Wordwise

colonist: person who lives in a colony

colony: community that belongs to a distant country

land: to arrive somewhere

A Safe Place.
After they landed, the colonists built a fort made of wood.

What Would YOU Take to Jamestown?

IMAGINE that it is 1607, and you are planning to migrate to Virginia. You will be one of the very first people to live in Jamestown. Very little is known about the place. Only a few people from your country have ever been there. What should you take along with you? What will help you live in this strange new land?

Is it hard to choose? Look at the photos on these pages. They can help you decide. These items belonged to real people who went to Jamestown in 1607. Scientists find these and many other things as they explore the original Jamestown colony.

HOUSEHOLD ITEMS

Bottle, Jug, and Jar. The Jamestown colonists brought dishes and other kitchen items with them from England.

TOOLS

Fish Hooks. The Jamestown colonists planned to catch and grow their own food. To help do this, they brought tools like these from England.

Scissors, Pins, and Thimble. There were no clothing stores in the New World. Colonists brought tools to fix their clothes instead.

PERSONAL ITEMS

Keys. There were no houses in early Jamestown. Colonists used keys like these to lock up their belongings in wooden trunks.

Toothpick. One colonist brought along this silver toothpick to keep his teeth clean.

Games. Life was hard in early Jamestown. But there was still time for games. These objects show that.

A Trail to Sail

Four hundred years ago, Captain John Smith made history. He explored the Chesapeake Bay. Now a national trail allows you to follow his adventures.

By Lana Costantini

IT IS NO SURPRISE that Native Americans lived near the Chesapeake Bay. The bay, which flows in Maryland and Virginia, is alive with wildlife. Crabs, oysters, clams, and fish live in the water. Deer, gray foxes, and minks live in forests nearby.

All those animals meant that people had plenty of food. Forests gave them wood for houses and cooking. So the population grew. About 100,000 Native Americans lived near the bay 400 years ago.

Exploring the Chesapeake

The Native Americans' world changed forever in 1607. A group of English people arrived. They built the fort at Jamestown, Virginia. It was the first successful English colony in all of North America.

One colonist was an explorer. His name was John Smith. He was the first European to explore the bay. Smith and his crew took several trips around the bay. In all, they traveled more than 4,800 kilometers (3,000 miles).

Old Ships. *These ships are copies. But they look just like the ones that brought the colonists to Jamestown in 1607.*

John Smith's Map. *John Smith made a map like this when he explored Chesapeake Bay.*

Tough Travels

Smith's trips weren't easy. He and his crew faced hunger, heat, and storms. Bugs bit them. Now and then, Native Americans attacked them.

Native Americans even captured Smith. He refused to obey their chief. So the chief gave an order to kill Smith. Then the chief's daughter spoke up. Her name was Pocahontas. She begged her father to let Smith live. The chief agreed. He later set Smith free.

Unexpected Treasure

Captain John Smith

Smith's brush with death didn't stop him. He and his men kept exploring. They searched for gold and silver. They also tried to find a way to Asia.

Smith didn't find what he was looking for. Yet he found a different treasure. That was the bay itself. Smith called it "a very goodly bay."

Sailing the Trail

Today, about 16 million people live near the bay. Cities stand beside rivers. Yet people can still explore the way Smith did.

In 2006, the U.S. government created the Captain John Smith Chesapeake National Historic Trail. It's the first national trail that people can sail on.

Trail Guide. *A "smart buoy" floats on the bay.*

The trail follows the same path as Smith's trips. Along the way, visitors learn about the Chesapeake Bay and the people who lived on its shores.

High-Tech Tour Guides

On the trail, visitors will find "smart buoys." A buoy is a floating marker. The buoys have recorded messages about the bay. The buoys also send out information. They tell about weather and water quality. People can get the information by phone or computer.

John Smith never found much gold. Trail visitors won't either. Yet they'll find the real treasure Smith found: an amazing place to explore.

You can visit the Chesapeake Bay buoys and learn more about the bay at buoybay.org.

∽—Happy Trails—∽

What's the best way to see America's natural beauty? Try walking, biking, and running its trails. Over 40 years ago, in October 1968, Congress passed the National Trail Systems Act. Its purpose was to make beautiful and historic trails for Americans to enjoy and learn from.

Today, national trails cover 80,000 kilometers (50,000 miles). They are in every part of the United States. They include the famous Appalachian Trail in the East and the Pacific Crest Trail in the West.

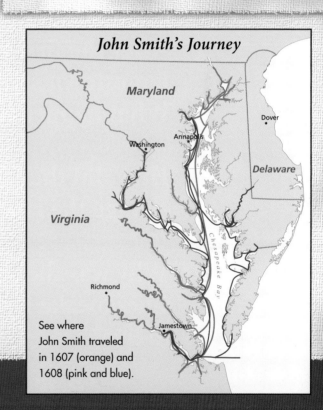

John Smith's Journey

Maryland

Dover

Annapolis

Washington

Delaware

Virginia

Richmond

Jamestown

Chesapeake Bay

See where John Smith traveled in 1607 (orange) and 1608 (pink and blue).

A New World

Get to know the Jamestown colonists.
Then answer these questions.

1 Why did the colonists build a fort at Jamestown?

2 After the first two years, life in Jamestown started to get better. What happened?

3 How did the Jamestown colonists change the land?

4 Why was the shore of the Chesapeake Bay a good place to live?

5 What is the Captain John Smith Chesapeake National Historic Trail? What can visitors learn from its "smart buoys"?